PERVERSE, ADVERSE AND ROTTENVERSE

By
June Foray

PERVERSE, ADVERSE AND ROTTENVERSE

By
June Foray

BearManor Media
2005

Perverse, Adverse and Rottenverse
Copyright © 2004 by June Foray.
All rights reserved.

Published in the USA by
Bear Manor Media

bearmanormedia.com

Cover design by Lloyd W. Meek
Typesetting and layout by John Teehan

Library of Congress Cataloging-in-Publication Data

Foray, June.
Perverse, adverse, and rottenverse / by June Foray.
p. cm.
ISBN 1-59393-020-8

1. American wit and humor. I. Title.

PN6165.F67 2004
818'.602--dc22
2004022211

ISBN 1-59393-020-8

To

My husband, Hobart Donavan, who clung to the myth that we had the "luck of the Irish", all bad.

Table of Contents

Foreword

If "virtue is its own reward", then who in this world of sophistication and fierce competition wants to cling to virtuosity with a pay-off like that?

"Love is blind." Absurd! Our flower children in the 60s dispelled that cock-eyed notion for a decade because of the evolution of various kinds of love—love for humanity, animals, peace and the great outdoors. Love has its eyes realistically open for the first time in our phrenetic world, and it's hanging right in there.

"Like father like son." Ho, ho, ho! Have you heard the far right, on gay guys lately?

I am resolutely determined to explode all the obsolete shibboleths that our parents drove into our adolescent, little minds, and I'm brazen enough to offer my, perhaps outrageous, judgment of the morals and mores of the establishment. It is my critique on society as it stumbled into the last quarter of the 20th Century and the first of our 21st, having lived by the myths given to us in centuries long gone.

June Foray [*signature*]

June Foray

June Foray

I looked around to find a pet

And liked the cow I never met

It was a duck that jumped the moon

And nothing happened much too soon

Nothing is as nothing does

It's buffaloes not bees who buzz

A mouse never did run up a clock

It's dogs that crow and not the cock

All cats survive by eating hay

Find icicles on a summer day

Do you know how the old woman feels

When the shoe that she lives in needs new heels

So much to do about something or other

Be kind to yourself and love your mother

If you don't understand this do or die

Don't worry, my friend, neither do I!

Never Speak III Of the Dead

Never Speak III Of the Dead

The please-don't-talk-about-me-when-I'm-gone syndrome idiomatic to the United States seems to persist, despite the expiration of our most notorious rogues. They pass on with silly symphonies of accolades whispered in the slumber rooms and receptions after the services. Sure, he robbed the poor, cheated the rich and kicked his wife around, but what the hell! He was a nice guy in his way.

So? Isn't everybody? If every human being weren't heir to foibles—surprise, surprise—we'd all be divinities, hiking around on the water, which would make for pretty clogged canals. Certainly, not everyone shuffling off this mortal coil is Mr. Good Guy, but you wouldn't think so by the eulogies. Mr. Nasty (or Ms. Witch) kicks the bucket, and there you are in the privacy of your own home sneering.

"It couldn't have happened to a nicer guy. Why did he have to wait so long?"

But what do you do when you get on the horn and call a mutual friend with the good news?

"Hey, did you hear? George just passed away."

Of course, we always pussyfoot THAT euphemism. Perish the thought we simply use the word "died". That's indelicate. Cowards that we are, we shrink from harsh reality whenever possible.

"Yes, poor George. And so young, too."

You can't bring yourself to betray your conscience and speak well of our non-hero—yet. But give you time. You have a few days to the funeral and multitudinous friends to visit before you

3

shape up and get around to being the hallowed hypocrite.

By the time you've been suffocated by the minister's pan-
egyrics, commiserated with the family and taken a last look at
the newly departed, you even believe your own crocodile tears.

"Terrific guy, wasn't he?"

Ah hah! Now you've graduated Pharasee cum laude, and
our own pariah in life has become a demigod in the great Never-
Never Land in the sky. How can you conceivably be irreverent?
After all, he's dead. And death commands respect. Balderdash!
Why?

Let's get down to bedrock. What is it in our society that
motivates our lavishing blandishments on apostates after their
demises when we despised their derelictions to humanity while
they lived?

Do we indulge ourselves in supernatural fears, or is it to
assuage our own feelings of guilt at possibly not fulfilling our
own lives? Perhaps we, in our unfaltering egos, wish to appear
as the compassionate friend who inspires grudging praise.

"I've never heard George say an unkind word about anybody."

It's your ego, chum. Ego pure and simple. How many times
have you attended a funeral because it was the thing to do, a
place to be seen, an occasion for you to expose an apocryphal
tear for the benefit of the mourners? Their depths of emotion
are probably equally as strained as yours.

So let's be blunt about it and call a gravedigger's spade a
spade. Don't be a smarmy Uriah Heep in your praise of male-
factors. If you wish to show mannerly politeness, shed your
tear, say nothing and keep your counsel. But be honest enough
with yourself to admit that you're glad that the rascal's gone,
and the devil take the hindmost. He's going to anyway.

WORKING LIKE A DOG

We all labor in our own particular vineyards. But like a dog? That cliché has seen its day — dog day, that is. Whether you're in a white-collar profession or blue-collar calling, the forty-hour-plus work week can become eventually a big, fat drag. And unless you're a dedicated, slick entrepreneur living the easy life, operating on your wits to gyp the next guy out of his honest bread, you're pretty glad to hit the road for home come the five o'clock martini whistle. The welcoming embrace of your faithful spouse is eclipsed only by the ebullience of your little four-footed canine friend, who hears you complain,

"Ho boy, did I work like a dog today!"

Who? What dog? Rover, who was wakened from his doggy dreams on your arrival? If he's a Dachshund, when was the last time that he dug the trenches for badgers? If he's an Irish setter, has he worked for his or your daily bread hunting recently? Since when has your Sheepdog herded wooly beasties in your backyard? The world "mush" in your vocabulary construes simply one thing, a morning cereal, not an order to your Malamutes to haul that sled through the crusty Alaskan snows.

Unique nine-to-five drudgery is endured in the United States by only two types of canine professionals, circus dogs and Lassie with his myriad stand-ins, who are obviously unaware of the long green hoarded in their owners' safe-deposit boxes. Their only conscious rewards are applause, an extra pound of meat and comfy bedrooms all their own. The Coogan Law doesn't even include provisions for a future college education for man's best friend. And as for the guard dog! Not only does he not receive remu-

5

neration but he rarely if ever hears a kind word from friend or foe.

But good ole Rover sleeps in your bed whether you're using it or not, takes rides to the beach, indulges in cat and squirrel chasing, bites the mailman and fecundates every bitch not restrained by the leash law. Fifth Avenue pups in Fun City even make the best-dressed list in their minks and diamonds. All fun, fun, fun! The only work of consequence accomplished by our furry pals is that of insinuating themselves to pacify and win over the hearts and minds of us willing peasants. Mission accomplished! But wouldn't you think that St. Bernards would have the decency to work for a living and fetch that cask of brandy to the depleted, work-weary office-holder at the day's end?

It beats hiring your Malamute to drag your sled from the railroad station to home. Especially in summer.

P.S. With apologies to Seeing Eye and drug-sniffing canines.

Beauty Is Only Skin Deep

A cautionary slogan if there ever was one, inferring in all probability that under each gorgeous epithelial layer beats a heart of stone, lie the conscience of an adder and mind of an amoeba. Foolishly, no one would deny that physical beauty IS only skin and bone-structure deep, as no one would deny, either, that minds like steel traps and the souls of saints don't give a damn what kinds of boxes they're wrapped in.

It's only been since the female of the species has emerged from society's womb that good-looking women have proven that they have the mental agility (as well as physical agility in bed) to enter politics, write books and sell them, edit magazines, whap a scalpel, pass the bar, open banks and expound on the living habits of chimpanzees, animal and human.

However, sadly, let's consider the less physically endowed but brilliant sister under the skin—or above or around it. Her endearing young charms are not perceived at the first handshake, and that's probably what she'll get, handshakes instead of kisses, until some not-so-dumb cluck of a man is captivated by her magic spell of character. Unfortunately, acceptance requires time with which no one can be profligate, let alone the Plain Jane who has been waiting too long as it is. One shiny example refuting this argument, however, is the demand for the ugly ducklings in television commercials. But who is financially well enough greased to hit the road for Hollywood or New York? Besides, not that many actors are working, including the beautiful people.

If, for example, two girls apply for one job as a receptionist.

Who will land it? The girl with the knock-out figure and baby blues, that's who. She may be fired for incompetence later and relinquish the position to brainy Ms. Unattractive, but guess what? Our lovely lady's proverbial foot-in-the-door trips an admiring employer with a paycheck in his eager, hot, little roving hands. Again I say that this doesn't imply that Handsome Hannas don't possess the wrinkles in the medulla oblongata or that brains are necessarily a concomitant to the unpretentious looking. It simply means that, regrettably, the world pays homage to classic pulchritude. Gray matter gallops in a poor second. The perquisite of the pretty face is the open sesame to employment, social intercourse (not forgetting the other kind, either), marriage. ANYTHING, like it or not.

Happily we've entered the era of plastic surgery where the lack of beauty can be corrected with a sharp knife and a few thousand bucks, paid in advance of course. Soooo, you little intellectual mousies, get that nose bob that you've always wanted, pop for a face-lift or skin peel, tell your avoirdupois to get lost. And heigh-ho to a stunning, exhilarating life ahead. It's right at the end of your new retroussé nose.

P.S. All of the above doesn't pertain to just the feminine gender. Males, also, are known to be trustworthy, loyal, helpful, friendly, kind, courteous, etc. etc.

Casting *Pearls* Before **SWINE**, Like

You won't hear Mikimoto Pearl Company calling,

"Here, piggy, piggy!"

You can bet your flitch of bacon on that. They're not going to have their pearl divers risking company yen in order to throw the oysters' contribution to society among piggeries the world over, when they know that they won't receive dime one. It's all a matter of Wall Street high finance. Swine don't have loose change hanging around their butts or spare ribs to pay off to the company store. All pigs can do is offer their bodies for payment. They do anyway, but not voluntarily.

And who says that swine would enjoy pearls particularly? What are they going to do with them, eat 'em? They're happier with old orange peels and leftover TV dinners. Also, the idea behind this old saw interprets itself to mean that not only are pigs gross physically, but their stupidity is even incredibly more so. Look it up! Pigs are known to have higher intelligence quotients than even man's best friend, and if their mental capabilities are as elevated as studies prove they are, they'd be nuts if they didn't prefer diamonds instead of pearls.

Secondly: this loathsome, Neanderthal adage infers that the ugly or mentally sub-standard human being isn't worthy of any significant beauty in his or her life. So, now you have not only the animal lovers and vegetarians ready for your jugular, you have the do-gooders and humanitarians at your throat. Even the most porcine individual enjoys, or should be privileged to enjoy, the splendor of a sunset, birds, a rose, a day without smog, and, yes, even a pearl. And unless the mercenary instinct prevails, we de-

9

light more in eating the oysters rather than cracking our teeth on the gems contained therein.

But let's get back to the intrinsic value of precious stones. Who was the dum-dum who conceived the idea that pearls were more attractive or expensive than diamonds—to cast even before swine? Any experienced gem dealer can irritate an oyster to form a perfect, natural, lustrous growth. But what or whom are you going to irritate for an exquisite diamond? Obviously, the poor black in South Africa working in the mines for a pittance as a quid-pro-quo for the joy of living in a squalid hut and a rap over the head for disregarding his curfew hour in white neighborhoods. But YOU pay the premium price for that good ole flawless, crystalline carbon. But leave us not become political. That is not our intent.

YAGS, you say? Of course they look like diamonds, but when you're down to your last credit card with its 18% interest over a period of a year, and your weekly stipend is non-existent, try to sell a YAG! The pawnbroker's heart will be as frigid as the Little Match Girl. Even a smart pig knows that.

So talk it over with your local swineherd before casting pearls before his charges. Or discuss the situation with someone who owns a pig as a pet. This intelligent animal, male or female, will prefer a diamond necklace or leg bracelet appreciably more—as will any woman prefer a diamond and not a pearl when it settles on her third finger, left hand.

One must conclude after analyzing this ridiculous slogan—don't malign swine.

Virtue

Is

Its

Own

Reward

Henry, the Eighth thought himself to be virtuous, but besides giving his wives headaches, all the rewards that he reaped were flatulency, bedsores and a rotten reputation. And give a thought to those sexually pure in soul and body, who join country clubs refusing admittance to minorities. Presumably they're rewarded by the assurance that their genetically saint-like daughters aren't going to marry any.

File card them with the holier-than-thou citizen to whom virtue means hitting the sack at bed time like a praying mantis.

"Now I lay me down to sleep ————," with spouse naturally and, of course, always with GOD. Freedom from social diseases is their primary bonus.

But horror of horrors! Consider the virtuous virgin, whose only recompense is being a virtuous virgin. Crawling in the hay at nighty-night with the Saturday Review in one hand and a Chihuahua in the other may be intellectually stimulating and kind to animals, but it's one lousy payoff for purity. Even if the aforementioned goody-goodies read Masters and Johnson, Fanny Hill or books on the joys of sex, their vicarious thrills are as tantalizing as a worm farm. Virtue is its own reward? Phooey!

Oddly enough, some convicted felons with their Robin Hood syndromes piously proclaim that they attempted to save their country from evil, fight just wars, combat communism and fascism, rob the rich to give to the poor and "protect" the investments of helpless widows to make them financially secure until they join their husbands in Nirvana. And what thanks did they get for their righteousness? A few years in the pen.

Too many self-indulgent people boast of their Polly-Anna-ish moral rectitude while at the same time displaying outrageous cupidity in being Polly-WANNA-ish. They wanna possess all the perquisites of wealth, wanna attain positions of power and fame. You can bet your bottom dishonest buck that they ain't achieving all those niceties by obeying the Boy Scout oath, that's a cinch. If you really reflect a minute—how many successful millionaires and multi-national corporations reached King Midas statuses by being anything other than Hard-Hearted-Henrys? Their diminution of virtue pays off better than the one-armed bandits in Las Vegas with yachts, Mercedes' and gorgeous mistresses whom they keep imprisoned in Caesar's Palace.

The aspiring Hollywood starlet, working under a famous producer, asks the mirror on the ceiling,

"Mirror, mirror, 'way up there, whom does this director think most fair?"

And the mirrored ceiling looks down in rapturous admiration and replies,

"Thou, who else? And, baby, have I got a thirteen-week TV series for you!"

It's ludicrous in this first quarter of the 21st century to equate sex with evil. But we do, and in our born-again Puritanical ethic, our most sophisticated consider it just another ho-hum bore.

So would-be, ersatz or bona fide sinners of the world unite. You have nothing to gain but tax-exempt bonds and nothing to lose but your virtue.

Imitation Is the Sincerest
Form of Flattery

Imitation Is the Sincerest
Form of Flattery

Rip-off! Rip-off! Whether it's sincere flattery all depends on the pecuniary status of the ripper and rippee. Ever see the security guards surrounding toy and doll factories on full 24-hour shifts in order to protect their new creations? Even though a prospective actor who voices mechanical dolls has a recording session, the obstacles for admission to the plants are worse than those encountered by foreign correspondents trying to visit the KGB nut houses. There's one helluva price to pay if a security guard pulls the string in his or her back and the actor doesn't give the passwords,

"Baby Go Poo-Poo!"

Any industrial or motion picture attorney worth his weight in caveats who actually believes this quotation garbage should drop dead. However, he's ecstatic if his clients are dumbbells enough to engage in imitation. Let's face it for what it is—stealing. His extricating them from litigation or the jug commands astronomical fees, which sustain him in his accustomed Cadillac and Paine-Webber dividends, while his obtuse clients (whether they win or lose their plagiarism cases) are suckered into Oliver Twist's poorhouse.

But ain't that just too bad. If they've knocked off others' inventions, they're bigger meatheads than suspected. Granted, the stakes are high if they can get away with it, but had they used the good old Medulla Oblongata (although no law says they gotta), there wouldn't be the necessity for a lawyer in the first place.

A digressing aside to the inglorious or otherwise: universities are matriculating lawyers as fast as the mythical box that ground its little sodium chloride heart out to make the ocean salty. More attorneys, more competition; ergo, less expensive services—er—maybe.

13

Las Vegas clubs and television recording studios shelter the latest ripper/rippee situations to come along the sound and video tape pike for years. Let's take Las Vegas first. That's a laugh! As though anyone could! Impersonators imitating other actors or public figures make four-digit salaries a week. Now, no one who has his marbles contests their talents, but what kind of shtick would they deliver if they were unable to do impersonations or find anyone to impersonate? Stale wife and mother-in-law jokes that are as humorous as kidney machines. Presumably, that's how the rippee feels. His impersonator gets the bread while he, the original, might be on his uppers, receives no royalties, no residuals. But hot damn, is he flattered!

There's no joy in Hollywoodville when an auditioning actor is confronted by a director or advertising genius looking for the voice of an anthropomorphic bat in an animated TV series.

"How's your W.C. Fields voice?"

Or Bert Lahr voice? Or Laurel? Or Hardy? Or Ed Wynn? You can bet your sweet glottis that this is an easy way out for the tunnel-visioned producer. The rippee can't protest; he's dead and couldn't use the money or flattery anyhow. Again Hollywood is living up to its reputation as being full of B.S. I beg your pardon. B.G.—Bat Guano.

"For the voice of the bee," suggests the director, "Try a Madonna."

Or Kirk Douglas. Look out! Here comes our friendly community lawyer again.

Oh, the indignity of it all: unimaginative employers who adhere to the above mentioned B.G. All it does is force the actors to wait for hours every two weeks in the unemployment lines practicing to be bees and sons of bees.

Where Ignorance Is B

l i s s

'Tis Folly To Be Wise

DIMWITS CAN BE BLISSFULLY WISE WHEN THEY CON-FRONT THEIR EGG-HEAD FRIENDS WITH THE FOLLOWING FACT THAT CONFOUNDS AND CONFUSES EVEN THEM. DROP IT IN CASUALLY WHEN THERE IS AN OMINOUS PAUSE IN CONVER-SATION.

STALAGMITES AND STALACTITES

WE HAVE STUDIED SINCE THE NURSERY.

STALAGMITES GROW UP FROM THE GROUND.

STALACTITES GROW VICE VERSARY.

Never Look a Gift Horse

 the Mouth

None of us is THAT ignorant concerning what this simple homily implies—never scrutinize or dissect generosity. And yet it'd be ridiculous to look into a horse's mouth for any reason unless, of course, he were a talking beastie who'd tell you what to bet in the sixth at Santa Anita. If you're curious about his age, leave the examination to your track-side vet who can probably give you a better racing tip than the one you heard straight from the horse's mouth. This philosophy of never looking a gift horse in the mouth smacks of the bon mots of some sniveling bookie, who doesn't know a horse's mouth from a horse's ass and doesn't want to know. The only horses' asses he counts on his tote boards are the knuckleheads who bet in the first place.

What gift, pray, can a horse offer, assuming that it's possible? It's a cinch, it's his cinch. Or it isn't from the mouth; so why look there? Kojak gets his puerile oral kicks from all-day suckers (Nielsens get theirs from the other kind at the receiving end of the tube). However, the more urbane of us are predisposed to be anal when we contemplate the rewards involved; therefore, let's probe the nether portion of the horse's anatomy where it's financially more appealing.

As opposed to the cement city of Manhattan, West Coast and suburban home owners are subject to the dubious delight of seeding, feeding or manicuring their lawns, and in Hollywood, as always, manure is big business. It hits the electric fan with regularity, especially in the advertising agencies, the competitive companies whom they represent and the actors who step on each others' faces to record their commercials. They all vie in their attempts to convince the bewildered lawn caretakers that their animals' feces are far superior for little stalks of chlorophyll than the others'. This is where the psychological clichés of being oral and/or anal insinuate themselves. Announcing a commercial for a manure company is most decidedly oral. Conversely, what could be more anal than the product? Offal is awful whether it's in the bag or just released by its creator, but ta-da! The actor receives overscale and all the instant organic fertilizer he can eat, while horsey continues to deposit his gifts ad infinitum keeping his anus open and his mouth shut.

Let's get out of the bathroom and into the bedroom, gift horses' trading center, the only relevancy to our equine equation being that these transactions occur while hitting the hay. Our cautionary advice is, by all means, take a good gander in your companion's mouth. Fourteen-carat crowns or rotting silver fillings are pretty accurate indications of whether his or her dietary fare was lobsters thermidor or Big Macs and, incidentally, of where your next meal is coming from. If the dental crockery is phony, chances are that your Easter Bunny has lived long enough to hoard a substantial amount of lettuce in Chase Manhattan, but watch out if the opposite exists! Social Security doesn't enhance your destiny with warm nights on the Caribbean or the French Riviera; it simply promises you hot nights under an electric blanket in a sleazy motel and next to a glass of water flavored with Dentu-Creme.

With an increasingly pugnacious Justice Department, certain Congressmen and Senators have flagellated themselves for not assiduously inspecting their hyperactive gift horse's mouth. They could have checked an advanced case of pyorrhea in a charming but lethal tooth fairy.

Many

Light

Many
Many
Many
Many
Many
Many

Light
Light
Light
Light
Light
Light

Many Hands Make Work Light

"Hail, hail, the gang's all here!"

What the hell do we care? Indeed! These many helpful hands should get their knuckles cracked, especially if they're bombarding the dining area like anti-personnel cluster bombs. Were sin-psyched Sigmund Freud alive today, his reaction to his guilt-ridden guests would be "screw 'em", and he had the couch to do it. But for the harried hostess—on the dining room table or portable dishwasher? Not hardly. Perhaps this less profane but defiant entreaty is more apropos.

"Don't just do something. Stand there!"

The Gaels of Ireland, who quake at the screams of the banshee presaging the death of a family member, ain't heard nothing' yet, until they hear the howls of reception givers bitterly denouncing their dinner guests, hoping that they *would* drop dead. And when the hosts along with the Farberware are too hot, be advised that that's the time to get the hell out of the kitchen. The vagrant thought of giving a dinner party for groups in excess of six is capricious in itself if individuals are impecunious enough to ill afford a maid, caterer or Melmac for eight. Lest we become too captious—bashes, with their concomitant saturnalia, can be fun.

When most people decide to entertain, they leave niggardliness behind with their Cracker Jack prizes and become the much-sung-about big spenders. Nothing but the most expensive brand-name mountain dew, cuts of meat and fromage savoisien. They put their best snoot forward.

The tab for the repast amounts to a couple of hundred smackers; so what? It's de rigueur, expected and accepted. It's the carnage created by comestible/alcohol-fatigued invitees who want to help clear the table later that leads to madness and tumescent Master Charge invoices. Where were all these do-gooders that morning when the hostess really needed their help scrubbing toilets? They wrap their slippery, palsied fingers around greasy plates and oops, there goes the Haviland. Even if grandmothers who bequeathed them were still alive, they could never replace their antiques. Heartbreak Hotelsville. Better to put the plates on the floor and let the sober family dog lick off the prime rib fat to a Windex shine. Although it takes a bit of crawling on all fours to retrieve them from under the dining room table where the dog has pursued them, presto! At least the china is intact and ready for the dishwasher. For holocaust numero uno, chalk up a stack of unexpectedly expended long green, if and when plates that even slightly resemble the pattern of the priceless set can be supplanted. Obviously, the bill in the china shop is far and above the initial cost of candlelight, booze and food generously and willingly served. This, however, is only the tip of the iceberg lettuce.

Although porcine creatures devour anything that doesn't contain arsenic, desserts slavishly concocted by innovative hosts customarily remain untouched by the abstemious. That's okay. Most hosts spurn those empty calories themselves. They appreciate that fact of life. What they don't appreciate is the many hands (supposedly making work light) scraping off the Baked Alaska and discarding it over the peripatetic waffle-weave dishcloth. Where else but inside the garbage disposal, natch. Disaster number two: an astronomical financial outlay for a new disposal. Another direct hit by the multi-national corporations, mothers' little helpers and the pleasant, pecunious, party-pooping plumber.

Calamity number three occurs when the valiant hostess plunges her hand in the water-filled sink where bread crusts and potatoes au gratin are floating like rubber duckies on the surface, and she finds what her kitchen assistants had hidden, the Wedgwood Irish crystal—hand cut. Hers! As if that weren't sufficient debasement, the final denigration intrudes itself when the guests play eeny-meeny-miny-mo to decide who will rush her to the emergency hospital for a tetanus shot and that stitch in time that saves nine. The clams served for hors d'oeuvres amount to a petty shell game compared to the one-hundred-and-fifty clams that she'll pay for medical expenses, a Blue double Cross.

Catastrophe number four can be dispatched with minimal exposition. How often have the hostesses, even with the mostestess-on-the-ball (or hosts with the mosts on the ——s) ignominiously fished around in the trash cans filled with watermelon rinds, chicken bones and wilted German salad, trying to find the Gorham sterling forks? They were, of course, inadvertently discarded by guests in haste to alleviate the burden of the entertainers and to get the hell home expeditiously because their baby-sitters' boyfriends have arrived at the zenith of titillation.

Only one segment of this bogus bromide's foibles has been explored here, but consider the contributions that a plethora of benevolent assistants can advance toward the mental derangement of, say, artists or accountants or writers or Santy struggling to navigate the chimney. The cruelest cut of all, however, is the devastation precipitated by excessive surf-side savants during mouth-to-mouth resuscitation. The multiplicity of eager lips and lungs usher with undue haste the demise of victims, delivering them with solicitude into the custody of the Grim Reaper. His work was made light, indeed. But then, on second thought, perhaps the expired will accept their dispatchments gleefully. Think of all the helpful souls who'll ferry them across the stygian waters to Hades, where for eternity they'll be reunited with all their long-gone, beloved, Hell-raising buddies. Considering the loneliness of the other place, where else would they rather be?

Honesty
Is the Best Policy

About 400 B.C., all of his neighbors and friends said,
"What's with this soap-headed Diogenes? He lives in a tub, and when he does get out of the bubbles to hike around the metropolis, he's always lit."

If the Corinthians had an energy problem, you'd never know it by the perpetual twenty-four-hour flame that Diogenes lugged around with him in an attempt to find an honest man. We know he wouldn't, couldn't, didn't in his threescore plus five, and after two thousand years, the poor deluded man is probably still spinning around in his own kerosene. Pursuant to the thought that probity is a thing of beauty, old Oedipus Rex refused to profit by the experiences of his beacon-bearing amicus; so he appeased his transgressions by plucking out his eyes when he ascertained the verities of family life. In the centuries following, what have we learned through his self-immolation? Incest is an incompetently naïve game plan to relate to relatives, and sanguinary martyrs, particularly blind ones, wind up on welfare. Perceptive knaves of today arrange their priorities. They scratch someone else's eyes out first.

Heavens to Ra, the canny Pharaohs of Egypt, who predated our idealistic Greeks, had mastered the con game with consummate ease, rejecting the dogma of do-gooders. Disgusting enough that, when their orgiastic lives concluded, precious jewels, golden thrones, gourmet viands, et al, were buried with the egomaniacal, self-proclaimed deities for after-life indulgences, why did they in addition feel compelled to murder all the hired help constructing the pyramids for their retention in bondage throughout eternity? Had Cheops leveled with his slaves, they would have flagged down the closest camel and clippity-clopped over to Mesopotamia. When they discovered the intent of their boss, it was too late. Their visceral reactions were already soaked in brine and interred along with their viscera in stone funerary vases. If they had only been aware when breaking their backs over the limestone project that they weren't even privileged to be born again through Osiris like their niggardly, empirical employer, they wouldn't have had their hearts in it either.

Despite the ardor of his penis erectus, the Pithecanthropus Erectus pithed off his fellow Pliocene troglodyte by cheating on the number of rocks that he exchanged in bartering for a mate. What else is new? The rocks in Machiavelli's head justified any means to accomplish his end. How déclassé and crude. Go ahead, curl your lip. Yet who's to say him nay considering the multiplicity of crafty rock-hounds abounding covertly today with, however, immeasurably more grace? Their upper-class, twenty-first century finesse keeps us fawning before their speciousness. On the bridal bed of government and finance, we actually think that we're being kissed while roundly being screwed.

Where would the good ole U.S. of A. and free enterprise be if the ingenuous Indians hadn't sold Manhattan for a few lousy beads, cunning sweet talk and a meretricious come-on by some Dutch subaltern's wife?

For the nonce, let's not even contemplate the little white lies of song and pen. By employing them judiciously, as does everyone, you can make a pig-in-the-poke feel as lovely as a sty-in-the sky; you can convince some dullard who invites you to a lackluster party that you really do suffer a case of infectious hepatitis and must stay in bed, when the truth is that you stay in bed but with a case of the hots for an intriguing and equally lustful companion. That's not dishonesty. That's class.

And who wouldn't pocket a cascade of coins that accidentally tinkles out of the telephone box after the initial deposit of a half a buck? Quite possibly it's a 300% profit. A minuscule pay-off, but the gratification of cheating Ma Bell with her astronomical bills for phone installations, unlisted numbers and message units between the hours of 8 A.M. and 6 P.M. remains nothing short of exhilarating. Then, too, the cost of mailing back the coins would exceed the joyous jackpot, and you know what Keynes said about deficit spending. Even Omar Khayyam's poetic perspicuity was right on target.

"Take the cash and let the credit go. Use it as a deposit on the nearest tent."

The above? Penny ante! But it seems redundant because of our profound knowledge through experience to reiterate or discourse on the mendacity of all concerned in freeway fender benders, drilling for oil, running for government, writing traffic tickets and autobiographies, fire sales, selling used cars and initiating assignations. DNA, the great chain of life, is reduced to a ring-around-the-rosy life chain of cupidity which, uniquely enough, appears to make us all winners in our hocus pocus society.

The naiveté of John Keats in his "Ode to a Grecian Urn" pays pitiful homage to an antiquated precept that honesty prevails—or should.

"Beauty is truth, truth beauty. That is all ye know on earth and ye need to know."

Too
    bad
       his
         Grecian
             urn
               has
      metamorphosed
   into
  a
  canopic
jar.

You Can't Teach An Old Dog New Tricks

Mebbe not, but you can teach 'em to a dirty old man and you don't have to be a costy prosti. Granted, his joyous participation may be only rheumy eyes and frozen hip sockets, but breathes there an octogenarian apprentice so dead that he's not eager to be escorted into the hay? Be sure, however, to take a needle with you into the haystack where it can be speedily found, filled with adrenalin, of course. The point is how many youthful sex kittens are sufficiently ardent to walk the fence at night and yowl for his desiccated body unless the geriatric fleshes out his Superman leotards with $100,000 bills?

After you've gotten him out of his fetal position on the couch and into his walker, overtly swallow a birth control pill, a ludicrous ancillary trapping that can stimulate his fading 1.5 battery libido. All you can get is merely the big C. A caveat for your codger—all of this must be planned for after lunch when he's had his gruel and nitroglycerin. By the end of afternoon, he's already on his way to replacing his pitiable 1.5 with an Eveready size D power cell and to leaping through the flaming loop like a man/woman-eating Bengal Tiger. Lancer maybe?

Just don't be dismayed if during your ear nibbling tryst, he retains his hearing aid and carpet slippers. Let him die happily with a run-down battery and his boots on.

Being a Dirty Old Man widower living in connubial bliss with a hot plate compounds his ineptness in the culinary arts, a fact known and exploited by fast food chains and father's friends, frozen food packages. Despite his mewling that

"Jane and Mumsie didn't do it like that!"

It's up to you in your generosity to re-educate the old canine to the joys of cooking—sex, the more paramount having been dispensed with in six not-so-easy lessons.

His prime trauma asserts itself on your monitior that he doesn't wield the same spoon for stirring and tasting. Although the social disease that he could have had years ago has long since dissipated, Hunter's Stew laced with Geritol and antacids is not an encouraging addition to Michelin's Guide to gourmet fare. An excruciating problem difficult to transcend is boiling spaghetti *al dente*, when he doesn't have a tooth in his head to test the result. If his senility and lack of 20-20 eyesight don't encroach upon his lessons, he can read the clock with the big hand and the little hand telling him that six minutes have elapsed. Avoid that pitfall. Be a big spender and buy him a timer. The bell not only informs him of the state of the spaghetti, but it wakes him up before both it and he are immolated. Another admonition! The recipes of your favorite cookbook aren't worth an Irish tinker's dam if the old roué permits his French roux to bubble over the burner to be ingrained forever in the precious, supposedly stainless steel.

Like Ivory Soap, 99 and 9/10 of your D.O.M.s have the energy, tenacity and volition to learn, accept and enjoy. If they don't, accept the futility. Close all the kitchen doors, his or yours, and leave the gas on under the soup. Simply blow out the flame. It's the only merciful thing left to do for both of you.

It's Better To Give Than To Receive

Instead of telling that to the Marines, tell that to a wealthy dowager, whose deceased husband left the bulk of his stocks and bonds to her and 154 for charity. Could be she despised the poor slob since the nuptial tie. The only thing she gave him was her womanly attributes when she didn't have a headache. Meanwhile, he thought she was niftier than a sniftier of gin while she plied him with pre-dinner martinis in a haze of candlelight and Napoleons with whipped cream for desserts. What was the speculation thundering around under that stiff purple coiffure?

"My, what great cholesterol and atherosclerosis you have! The better to kill you with, my dear." Subtle? Not very. It's too commonplace. He was about to hit the skids anyway; all she did was to expedite it a few years prematurely so that her heart could belong to another richer, older daddy, who would just need a gentler shove to meet his predecessor. Then off to Las Vegas on a date with a cold one-armed bandit and a warm two-armed lover.

Alms, alms for us poor consumers who are bombarded inexorably by media advertising.

"With a gimme, gimme here, and a gimme, gimme there. Here a gimme, there a gimme, everywhere a gimme, gimme." Especially on Mother's Day. All the advertisers will get from a single gal and/or childless wife is a contemptuous lip as curled as ringlets made by an electrical hair-shaping wand. She receives neither felicitation, flower, feeling nor farthing one, but boy! Does she give. Captious though you may be, come on, admit it. Couldn't she, being a woman, at least be Mom-for-a-day and get a "here, here" instead of a "gimme, gimme"? Not does it only blow the bachelor girl's cash flow but it blows her mind to receive wearyingly incessant invitations in the mail to give.

"The stork is going to bring a little baby-poo to the Jones household. Please attend our shower and share the joy."

What the hell, she didn't share the sybaritism in conceiving the wee one, why share the dubious pleasure of paying for its didies?

The always-the-bridegroom-but-never-the-bride coughs up blood every time she coughs up shower gifts for her multitudinous girlfriends joining the ranks of wedded bliss. What thanks did she get? Years ago she joined the blanks of the unbedded miss. Kindly tell, what did she ever receive for that? More invitations to give wedding presents to the baby (whom she helped pay for) born to the Jones family twenty years before.

But ah, the honey-bunnies. There's another story. The little that they give to their lover-boys they enjoy giving away for free anyway. Who doesn't? But it's not a donation, my friend. The quid-nuncs can quote the quid-pro-quos of the cuddly concubines, condominiums and Cadillacs. Not bad for piecework.

Let's not even indulge in any lengthy dissertation on the Sunday morning evangelist. His reconditeness is so non-existent that you don't have to ask whether it's better to give than to receive. All he has to do is cast his rectitude upon the airwaves, and the bread that comes back buys a helluva lot of wine and fishes.

NEVER PUT OFF UNTIL TOMORROW WHAT YOU CAN DO TODAY

Oh, the ecstasy, the delirium of procrastination! "Today" you can shop for a new Pierre Cardin creation, visit Disneyland or seize the most convenient paramour for love in the afternoon. You can feel as free as a mini-pad. But holy moly, stay away from television if all you can watch is "Search for Tomorrow". Why carry the lantern around like our Greek pal looking for tomorrow? Its inevitability is always with us when we ante up to Carte Blanche for our excesses, go to court, suffer through a lower G.I., fight the I.R.S., pick up our kid for the weekend and pay the piper.

Why didn't dumb cluck Chicken Little procrastinate until the next day to alert the barnyard that the sky was falling? Because it never did, she almost found herself in a pot of Jewish penicillin and daffy Ducky Lucky at the end of Chairman Hua's chopsticks.

More proof? There's that saccharin simpleton Snow White. When the witch offered her the glowing poisoned apple, she could have remembered Weight Watchers and said,

"No thanks, I've already had a banana today. I'll wait until tomorrow to eat the apple."

But then, Snow White was so stupid that she couldn't even count to seven unless she had the dwarves around. Also, the gorgeous step-mother/witch with her magic ward could have ordered Snow White to do the housework, ensuring that her klutzy stepdaughter would break the magic mirror enslaving her to seven years of rotten luck. SW would have graduated moron-cum-laude and been able to at least count to 14 by this time.

Like all the rest, one who catches the kewpie doll with a dunce cap is Giddy Goldilocks. Not only does she frolic through the woods all by her lonely, but she helps herself to the bears' cottage, cottage beds and cottage cheese. The second was the goof. Balmy Bleachhead should have mucked around a little longer with her porridge and procrastinated until the homecoming. Instead of frolicking in Papa Bear's bed all by her lonely, she could have had a romp in bed with Papa Bear.

For over three hundred years, how could none but rave on the Bard of Avon? But if you want to put a pound of flesh on the bare Capulet, you can parlay one of his goofs into a hey-nonny-nonny. So maybe Friar Laurence was derelict in getting the scoop to Romeo that Juliet had swallowed a 48-hour Nembutal. When Romeo enters the tomb of his beloved thinking her D.O.A., why couldn't he at least have called the personal Montague paramedics, Friar Laurence or applied mouth-to-mouth resuscitation. That worked before. Couldn't he have restrained his rashness for at least a couple of hours? Until tomorrow? But no! He knocks himself off with rapid dispatch, quaffing the apothecary's poison. Bereaved Juliet, instead of awakening to orange blossoms and the lark, finds a dead duck and plunges herself into eternity with Romeo's bare bodkin into the depth of her cleavage, which transcends the depth of her brain.

II, IV, VI, VIII, learn thou to procrastinate!

Socrates could have put off until tomorrow what he did the day before, drinking the hemlock precipitously, because the fall of the Roman Empire wasn't too many tomorrows away. With his good health, he could be alive today. Ask Eddie Gibbon. Gibbon delayed for a few centuries to write about it, his estate still reaping the royalties. Gibbon fiddled while Socrates burned.

So be advised through the folly of Chicken Little, Goldilocks, Rummy Romeo, et al, that it's "tomorrow the world", which includes your oyster-on-the-half-shell—with a pearl.

MON£Y TALKS

Not in government statistics.

IT'S OIL OR LABOR COSTS OR FOOD
OR FLUCTUATING RENT.
INFLATION'S ONLY, SO THEY CLAIM,
ONE TENTH OF ONE PERCENT.

Pride **Goeth** Before a F
a
l
l

By latest account, Mr. Bean not only retains his pride, but he has acquired a pot as well.

MERRILL LYNCH, FENNER AND SMITH

'S A KNOTTY NAME TO CONJURE WITH.

I CAN'T FORGET IN ALL THAT JAZZ

THAT MR. BEAN IS NOW A HAS ———.

Vanity, Thy Name Is WOMAN*

(With an apologia on an ode to myself or any other woman)

I'M NOT A DULL, UNCOMELY LASS

LACKING BREEDING, POISE AND CLASS.

THOUGH WORLDLY WISE, I'M EVER SWEET

WITH SHAPELY FORM ALTHOUGH PETITE.

MEN DO FIND ME MOST DISARMING,

BRILLIANT, LOVELY, TRULY CHARMING.

SUITERS LOVE THE GENTLENESS

AND WINNING GRACE THAT I POSSESS.

WHEN CONVERSATIONS TURN TO SHADY

MY SAVOIRE FAIR BEFITS A LADY.

I BLUSH AS DOES THE ROSE IN BLOOM

AND INNOCENTLY LEAVE THE ROOM,

BUT ALL THE VIRTUES OWNED BY ME

ARE EXCEEDED BY MY MODESTY.

* B.S.

Haste
Makes Waste

"HURRRRY, HURRY, HURRY! Get your red-hot used car here. Not a scratch—like new—mint condition. You get more gas from a baking soda bromide than you use in this beautiful vehicle."

Where have you heard this before? You wrote the book, kiddo. Your own Blue Book. P.T. Barnum was the smart-ass with his quote,

"There's a sucker born every minute and two to take him."

No profound Aristotelian philosophy that. Nevertheless, it makes you gleeful that your mother made you a dual personality, but sorry that you don't have a clunker a minute to sell.

You just bought a new car, and you're not going to be the dumb nut who turns it in to the dealer. We all know what you'll get, don't we? They know a piece of junk when they see it. So do you. But the sucker who buys it doesn't. You hike to the Five-and-Ten-Cent Store and buy a For Sale sign for five—bucks that is. While you're plastering your telephone number on it, your mechanic is filling your radiator with Never-Leak and the motor block is oatmeal. If the new owners can't drive the car, they can eat it. But be hasty, my friend. With check in hand and the pink slip signed away, get it to hell out of the driveway, and you're home free. The buyer of your heap doesn't even get home.

Having enjoyed a free, unobtrusive lunch of apples, mushrooms and Twinkies secreted into their tummies to fortify secretions necessary for possible confrontation by the manager or police, supermarket petty pilferers laden themselves to the deltoids with blade-cut shoulder chops and to their hocks with ham of the same latitude. Weighing twenty pounds more than when they sauntered in, our porcine plunderers take the lamb on the lam and make a hasty exit through the quick-check stand paying only for the paperback "How I Made a Million in the Market" and a bottle of aspirin. Too bad! They could have lifted some needful brains and heart from the meat counter.

Take the fences who buy stolen objects like typewriters, television sets, musical instruments and classy jewels. You think that they, in their turpitude, don't unload them with fastidious haste? Haplessly, sometimes into the hands of undercover fuzz.

Then,
and only then,
does the fence get it in the part
that went over the fence
last
and becomes a prospect
for the

Hasty Pudding-head Club.

A Stitch In Time Saves Nine

IX

ATTEMPT THE WRITTEN DRIVER'S TEST?

YOU'LL GET JUST PASSING GRADES AT BEST.

ONE CAN'T DECIPHER ALL THAT FUZZ.

EXPIRE BEFORE YOUR LICENSE DOES.

It's a Small World
It's a Small World
It's a Small World
It's a Small World
It's a Small World
It's a Small World

COLUMBUS AND THE SCHOLARS FOUND

THE WORLD ON WHICH WE DWELL IS ROUND.

BUT NEO-CLASSICISTS DECLARE

LIKE, MAN, THIS BALL OF WAX IS SQUARE.

Every Day In Every Way
I'm Getting Better and Better

"One, two, up, down.
Touch your toesies with your nosies."

Take care of that body, baby. Unless you believe in reincarnation, it's the only one you have hangin' around, although we all know that there are sinister miscreants around relentlessly conducting you into a catatonic state through one malady after another. And you are blissfully oblivious.

Happy the era that you found mercury only in thermometers. Now, you're downing it internally in your eight glasses of drinking water every day. Despite the hazards, it's convenient to know when you have a fever and are growing a couple of inches taller at the same time. Does the Department of Health, Education and Welfare clean up our H_2O from industrial dispersions? Hell, no! They're just as bovine as we and drink out of the same trough.

The hysteria of keeping fit pervades every household, not just yours. The only incidents in which you ever saw citizens running before are when they were being pursued by the opposite sex or escaping from the scene of the accident. Did you ever see so many jiggling genitals, the owners of which are wearing them thin running around the streets, parks and playgrounds? Pump that blood! Expand those lungs! Breath a little carbon monoxide, refiners' effluents and you might be fortunate enough to land under a tent of pure oxygen in intensive care. But you're a health nut fiercely intent on getting more lead in your pencil. Well, get the smarts. Stop running, desist, lay off! Concentrate on your gluteus maximus and getting the lead out.

Like all good marathoners, before you spend 9:00 to 5:00 licking the world, you're going to eat the nourishing cereal that all champions eat, the one containing every vitamin from here to breakfast—plus BHA and BHT. It's the wheat flakes that are going to be preserved forever on your shelf, not you. You'll just be on the shelf.

45

For lunch, instead of brown-bagging apples, oranges, bananas or Bugs Bunny carrot sticks, you settle for the deli delivery of either a pastrami or corned beef sandwich. All protein and amino acid, right, on no preservative rye? If you think that all work and no play makes Jack a dull boy, be fore-warned that all work, cholesterol and nitrosamines in those cold cuts make you duller, Jack. Every day in every way you're getting deader and deader. The daily deli makes the jack.

To the exhortation of every elegant beauty salon in the U.S. and Paris, the search by creatures of both sexes for the fountain of youth grinds on. Heav-ens to Beauty (The Beast ingests his own "ugly" formula), don't ever scrub your face with soap and water! Smoooooooth those exorbitantly costly emollients into that crusty epithelial layer of your face to cleannnnnnnnssse and soffffffftiennnnn. Open those pores with titanium dioxide, aluminum stear-ate, quaternium-15, serine, bensoin, phenoxyethanol, methylparaben and D & C Red no. 17 and 19, everyone's favorite cream to recapture youth, loveli-ness and poverty. It's more efficacious to lather with soap and imbibe milk of magnesia. Keep those pores closed and your bowels open. But what the hell! At this stage of life, relax. If the chemicals don't getcha, the A bomb will.

A Trilogy

3

TURN THE OTHER CHEEK

Read your cinema history. Mae Clarke took a grapefruit in the face from that swell brute of a lover, Jimmy Cagney. She nobly turned her other cheek and still got the squirt from the squirt. Rhett Butler was socked with the old one-two from Scarlett, asked for more and got it. Took a slow burn in Atlanta, then chucked it all and didn't give a damn. Well, our 21st Century gal doesn't relish turning the other cheek after she's been slapped, most particularly when her back is turned—even on the classy Via Veneto. Conversely, for the male transvestite, the more open-handed blows the better, but that's another Brothers Grimm story.

He or she has to be some kind of a Keystone Kop, who when he/she gets it in the chops, stands there and says,

"Thanks, I needed that. Land me another."

Oh, the pie in the face is forthcoming, all right. But he/she didn't need it. He/she deserved it.

And whither go the mental maunderings of the self-indulgent masochist, whose boyfriend tells her to go jump into Lake Michigan and who, when she comes back, finds him gone? Then turns the other water wing and jumps into Lake Erie. As long as she's dumb enough, she'll always endure close encounters of the turd kind.

When she's not flashing around on her spiked sandals at highly frequented watering places, the lady-of-the-evening usually takes it lying down on both posterior cheeks. She figures that munificent remuneration transcends humiliation. Ah, but when it comes down to settling with her cheeky procurer, and takes it on both fleshy sides of her head, grins and bears it. Even reaches into her Gucci boots, guilelessly pulls out a couple of hundred in hidden profits and says,

"Here, how can I hold out on a sweet sonuvabitch like you?"

Apparently, the only tricks in which she's accomplished are relegated strictly to the four-poster.

None of us is left unscathed by some contemptible, car-cruising cop, who must bulldog it to the police oath of being uncompromising merciless to the motorist. Gotta get that mota quota. He selects you and thousands like you for an unjustified moving traffic violation. Not unlike the gay caught in a compromising position, you accept his charge of "following too close". You know that you're inculpable; but worse, you're servile. Reaching too quickly for the license in your wallet may very well be misconstrued as reaching for a gun. In that case, you might not only be taking the whole disgusting matter lying down, literally in the road. Your subservience could be rewarded by your becoming simply another statistic on the obit pages.

So live the university song "Fight on, ———," give it the old college try, go to court, sue City Hall, scream bloody murder, blow the whistle, challenge that recalcitrant assertiveness of yours. Should you discover that your dominant docility still remains resolute by being on the receiving end of a right to the chin, just turn your other head. The one with the hole in it.

GRIN AND BEAR IT

See above.

LAUGH, CLOWN, LAUGH

See above.

It Takes One To Know One 1

Larceny is a many-splendored thing, which more often than not always strikes in the same place simultaneously. One crook, like the right hand and the left hand, doesn't know what the other crook is doing, let alone recognize him. Thus, he's frequently kayoed with both the left and the right hands, which do know what they're doing.

"Hey, Taxi!"

The clarion Tarzan cry from here to Nairobi.

"Another out-of-town sucker. What does he know from this berg?"

With the price of gasoline accelerating, Crooked Cabbie vacillates between meter and litre. The meter wins clock-hands down; so he doesn't turn it on. What he does turn on is the charm, his cupidity becoming the Cupid for his crooked arrows. C.C. gasses about the noo art museum. Ain't Central Park gorgis in summer? See the pretty birdie! In the meantime, his hayseed fare in the rear sits smugly unaware of his imminent shafting. At the passenger's destination, Crooked Cabbie recoils with sanctimonious self-revulsion explaining the I-forgot-to-turn-on-the-meter bit.

"My fault. I'll give you five bucks off what it's supposed to be."

The fare grins good-naturedly. Fare is fair. C.C.'s eyes light up like the Star Trek computers on the starship Enterprise.

"Shucks, it could happen to anybody. This twenty ought to do it. And keep the change."

Hayseed makes a quick exit out of the taxi and into his silk-lined suite. Maybe Crooked Cabbie has just come down from an exhilarating space jaunt. Hellion Hayseed has just come fresh from the counterfeiters.

Myriads of swingin' singles are being left at the bar's swingin' doors because they ultimately discover that their pardners not only have spouses, but are going to marriage counselors to fortify their connubial bliss with them. The modern wife is hip to her husband's monkey business trips by this time, but the Cartier caches at the end of them mollify her anger, keep her tongue leashed and secure her economic future through their 50th wedding anniversary.

And the women masquerading as singles? Would that they had the lecherous husbands instead of the low-sex-drive louts they have, whose interests gravitate to TV, Monday Night Football and low-brau beer. No Tiffany titillations for them. All they wind up with are the Skittles. So off with the wedding rings and on with disco décolleté, which becomes more so after the ball is over and another one just beginning with their new singles. If they are singles. It takes one to know one? The only single we're certain about is the Pope.

Swapping partners is definitely in now with the bang gang. Wifey has her matinees; hubby has his evening lays. Guilt confronts guilt; however, when neither is remotely cognizant of the swap. So they bill and coo overtly while they grill and stew in their hair shirtly.

Does one cheapskate know another cheapskate? Not until the check at the restaurant comes and sits on the plate through the coffee, after-dinner drinks and post-prandial lethargy.

It takes one to know one? Unless he's come out of the closet, one gay can't be sure about another until he's found cruising on Santa Monica Boulevard. One white-collar pariah can't tell another white-collar piranha until the attack.

So, if you think that one villain knows another villain, get out your magnet. You've got a screw loose somewhere.

The Early Bird Gets the Worm

If you're a pea-headed, feathered, flying vertebrate, you don't have to split your nest at the crack of down to find your favorite maggot. Just fly through the window of a gourmet restaurant kitchen to assuage your delicate taste buds with varietal feasts of annelid larvae. At your convenience! A.M., P.M. or stratagem. There are enough to go around from her to the Health Department. Should you be, however, like the hairless, two-legged cuckoo who kicks the covers before daybreak in search of his lullaby of birdland, consider yourself more feather-brained than you think.

Attempting to surpass logic of the establishment requires more than an early-to-rise mentality, which frequently backfires with the pack-er-peck of the genus Tyrannus Kingbird. Take inveterate, megalopolistic U.S. travelers who pay top cabin all the way from their floral-scented sheets and three-bath homes to the primitive habitats in exotic lands east and west of the International Dateline. Dragging wheeled luggage packed to zippers with underarm deodorants, hairspray and Lomatil, they hit the skyways in possession of virginal expectations and hygiene, but our peripatetic early-bird friends disappointingly encounter their initial trauma aboard the 747. As soon as the "no smoking" signs fade to black, they rush to initiate the toilets before others violate them, the washbasins and the floor. Should they be insolent enough to elbow their kidneys to the head of interminable lines of anxious men and women (anti-E.R.A.ers, take note. Both sexes use the same facilities. Unfortunately for the lascivious, not simultaneously), they find themselves in the freshly scrubbed lavatories so pristine that they don't yet include necessary appointments like tissue, rolls or facial. Above and beyond that deprivation, their mommies haven't pinned hankies on their turtlenecks. They have two alternatives: suicidally eliminate eliminations or, since they're not the first creatures on God's green earth to elimi-

51

nate, at least be first to eliminate being first.

Wouldn't you think by this time that these worm-eaters would get the message? You can wager your sweet nest egg that they haven't. Our bird-brains are outsmarted again at their hotel when they angle to crash through the queues of other fatigued jet-laggers only to discover that the nest hasn't been vacated by the previous birds, who had gotten worms eating rancid Chicken Kiev at an early dinner. Our early-bird gets the worms—angle.

They roll out of bed by 5:30 the next morning dragging their frigid derrieres behind them into the bathrooms as cold as Yellowstone National Park in winter. The blue-lipped geezers are expecting steam-heated geysers, and they're going to have their hot tub baths before the steam runs out of the faucets or them. Don't they know that these energy-saving countries haven't even turned on the water heaters yet? Our early-birds wash their wings in icy-water tubs. So the tubs get the rings and the E.B.s suffer with what they chirped for in the first place—ring worms.

Good old Dan'l Webster's definition of a worm is a human being who is an object of contempt, loathing or pity. When push comes to shove, in being first, the worm usually gets the bird.

All's Well That Ends Well

Right on!

Right on!

Right on!

Right on!

Right on!

Right on!

Right on!

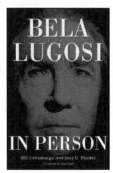

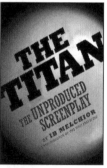

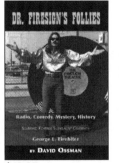

DISCARD

Made in the USA
Lexington, KY
01 August 2017